AF230045

My Mind at the Break of Day

M. E. Hicks-Singh

authorHOUSE®

AuthorHouse™
1663 Liberty Drive, Suite 200
Bloomington, IN 47403
www.authorhouse.com
Phone: 1-800-839-8640

First published by AuthorHouse 8/25/2008

ISBN: 978-1-4389-1062-8 (sc)

Printed in the United States of America
Bloomington, Indiana

This book is printed on acid-free paper.

Poems are written by inspiration. Some poets are inspired by life experiences both personal and impersonal. Others write by inspiration of love, discouragement, despondencies, nature and even divine inspiration.

Millie Singh is a poet that has written poems to fit many occasions both secular and religious.. She has written poems that will inspire you and cause you to think about life with your family and about others who you care about. She inspires a person to pick up a pen and attempt to write poems based upon their own inspiration about life, family and other things that they deem important in life.

The poems in this book will inspire you and make you think and at the same time wonder how was she able to pen what was in her heart when we're not able to say what's in our heart many times over.

As her senior pastor, mentor and unpublished author I am proud to have the opportunity to write this foreword because I believe in Millie Singh and her gift to write such wonderful poems for the world to read.

Van J. Alexander
Sr. Pastor, Christ Kingdom Church in Dallas, Tx.

I have spent 33 years of my life at the feet of a very wise woman. This wise woman is Millie Evelyn Hicks Singh, my mother. I am very excited that she is sharing her wisdom with the world in this book of poetry.

This book will give the reader strength and hope in times of trouble. It will also remind the reader of the importance of the family in poems such as My Daddy, No Secret What A Real Mom Can Do, Fearfully-Wonderfully Made and A Singular Purpose Of A Life.

She is able to use the written word and take the reader on a delightful journey into her mind, heart and spirit.

I pray you do not look at this book as just another book of poetry. I pray that the wisdom in this book leap from the pages and is able to be applied to your life.

I will leave you with a quote from her poem, Not Today, so be at ease guard your place, meet life head on face to face, when adversity comes your way let your answer be Not Today, Not Today.

Thanks Mom for the ride.

Your loving Son, Tom Runnels

Praise be to God for My Mind at the Break of Day:

I have many to thank and appreciate: (bio)
My Mother and Father the Late Frank & Ira Lee Hicks, who have always stood up for me and encourage me to do my best in whatever I decide to do as long as I go with God. I dedicate this book of poetry to them and to my brother the late Frank Lee Hicks Jr. I thank God for many family members that always encouraged me but they are too many to name. Thanks to My Pastors Van & Jackie Alexander who always gives me encouraging words stating just do it. I have a great Bishop that has written a great book name Late Bloomer, Bishop David E. Martin along with the gem of his life, the first Lady of Gospel Tabernacle Church here in Dallas. Bishop's book really gave me a boost to get started on my book of poetry. To my church family such a lovely group of people, Christ Kingdom Church, I say thanks for listening to me whenever I introduce one of my poems to you, I felt really encourage knowing you were interested and you really cared for my writings. God has really been good to me, I was born in 1946 which makes me 61 years old now and I'm publishing my first book as the saying goes better late than never. But by the time this comes out I will be 62 years old. I've met a lot of good people in my life and they all have had some influence on me. I've made some good decisions, some great ones and some not so good ones and they all have brought me to this place in my life. I've chosen to learn from all mistakes I've made and turned my life around to be a beacon of life and hope to someone else. I was raised in Garland, Tx. From the very early age of 4 years old. Born in

Dallas, Tx . at the age of 4 my parents bought their first home in Garland. I have three wonderful children who no matter what has always been there for me. I thank God for them Robert Te'Darin Runnels my oldest, Ira Danielle Runnels my middle one and Tommie Nakia Runnels my baby. I have two of the best Daughter-in-laws, they are very supported of me also, I've got to name them Latonya Runnels and Dezondria Runnels. I'm blessed to have nine grandchildren, thanks guys and girls for putting up with granny so much. I must name them. From the oldest to the youngest. Rayshawn, Davonte', Jamarcus, Jordan, Jasmine, Justin, Jaylen, Tommie Jr. and Evelyn.

Seasoned Voices

Dedicated to Seasoned Saints Community Choir:

Voices sprinkled with wisdom,
experience with joy and sadness;
given over to much gladness.
Age does not matter it is what's
Taken from it that will cause a clatter,
Strengths of old, turned into words of gold.
Seasoned voices offered lots of choices.,
Singing the glad tunes; even when clouds cover,
and it looks like you're doom. A smile of
sunshine rays makes the difference in your days.
SEASONED voices keep on going, with a never
Ending sound, for someone needs to hear and feel
What they have to say, whether they be up or down.
Age does not matter it is what's taken from it
That can cause such chatter.

As One

With my eyes lifted upward;
I see the gift of Unity.
Towards people is,
Standing in separate places;
For all races,
We were pre-destined to be,
The pride of being we,
Whom has an ear let them hear;
The sweet bells of life cheer.

Unconditionally Love

Dedicated to Pastors Van & Jackie Alexander

There are many ways to say, I love you;
There's many ways for love to shine thru,
But there's only one way for love to be;
That is to Love unconditionally.
Love, when friends are many;
Love, when you're lonely and haven't any,
Love, without resistence;
Love, with consistence,
Love, without gain;
Love, thru life's pain,
Just Love unconditionally.
Love, who seems unreachable;
Love, who seems unteachable,
Love, the unbearable;
Love, the unreliable,
Just Love unconditionally.

No Secret What a Real Mom Can Do

There's no secret, what a real Mom can do;
She'll cry with you, while you're going thru;
She'll confer in prayer, to the Father above,
Standing in the gap, full of love.

No Secret, what a real Mom can do.
No Secret, how far she'll go for you;
Walk through life walls, all thru your falls.
Day or Night always on call.

Validated by God, Gifted by His touch,
Mark with His kindness, gentleness as such.
Appreciative, instinctive and true,
A heart of gold, that can't be sold;
It's No Secret, what a real Mom can do.

No Secret, No Secret, Love you Moms!

A Singular Purpose of A Life

Dedicated to Darin, Latonya, Danielle, Tommie,
Dzondria

Adoration of a life being borned;
Animation of a life, lived and worned,
Manifestion of a life made known;
Comes the elation of a life, well adorned.

A life well planned, is a life in demand;
A life with intent, is full of investment.

A singular purpose of life,
Uttered under a divine inspiration;
Becomes a design transformation,
Duplicated by twos, threes, and fours,
Will allow you to walk thru many doors.

The Eyes

Dedicated to My Mother Ira L. Hicks
And Bishop David & Melanie Martin
Of Gospel Tabernacle of Dallas, Tx.

Eyes are the windows into the soul;
Where the different colors shows
Only the family ties. But the soul
Is colored with truth or lies,
Whether they're green, black, hazel
Or blue, light or dark brown too, you
Can see lightness or darkness that
Stands out bold. You can see the
Strengths and/or weaknesses that are
Forever to be told. Look into the eyes
Where the real truth shall arise.

Which Way

Which way is up
Which way is down
I fill wasted and about to drown

Which way do I run
Which way do I turn
I'm in the state of no concern

Do I go left
Do I go right
For my life looks a mess at first sight

What do I do
Whom do I seek
Can there really be any help for me?

Just Because

I pledge a life of change not to complain;
Not to be burden with life's rain, not to
Sing a sorry song' but swift in my thoughts;
Swift in my giving, swift and driven, not
Given to naught, just because.

I pledge a voice of reality, not formality;
Not to be unkind, not to lose so much time;
Swift in my giving, swift and driven, not
Given to naught, but swift in my thoughts,
Just because.

Planted By Still Waters

When the wind comes and the waters rise.
We will stand like a tree,
Planted by the still waters.
Trials and tribulations will come;
They may shake us, but God's hands,
Will keep us. We shall stand like a tree;
Planted by the still waters.

We are planted, like a tree;
By the still waters, things may shake us;
But God's hands will keep us, for we
Are planted like a tree; by the still waters.

Set Free

In life' ocean and about to drown,
Been tried in life's fire and thrown around;
Just then I saw, the parting of my sea, I
Have been set free. I will never ever be
The same; no longer walking, as if I'm
Drained, while standing by the living water,
Like a strong tree, not allowing my situations
Speak for me; I've been set free. My trust is in a
Higher power. In the midst of this very hour.,
My self has no wealth my thoughts are of good health
I now claim much peace; I have the victory, for
I've been set free. Free, Free, Free, Free;
You step in and set me free.

Chronicles Of A Quilted Life

Let the fruits of my lips speak passionate,
While abiding with strength;
Full of compassion, being up close and
Personal with thy brother,
Reaching back for a brother.

Forewarned is to be forearmed where
Thy eyes must take thee,
While a sister honors a sister,
With adoration, having a direction;
For a fragmented life, as a vessel,
Full of benefits with a great;
Connection, lay broken, with a shallow
Breath, with a life magnified,
Yet alive in the patterns; of
Quilted lives.

A Quilted Life Rest Faithfully in the
Shadow of colors:

My Daddy

To Father's that knew how to be a Daddy!

You never were too tired, to stop by my crib;
You never were too tired to tickle my rib.
You took time out of your days, showed me
Love in so many ways, for me you was always
There, holding me up before God in prayer.
I could not have ask God, for a better pappy;
than what he provided me with you as my daddy.
You taught me how to stand tall, you showed me
How to get up from a fall; you supported me in
All that I did, you never once made me felt I
Should have hid. I'm proud to be kin to you,
I'm proud to say my daddy too; I'm proud God
Gave you to me, I'm proud and happy as I can
Be. There's nothing that I would not do, to
Continue your teachings to my children too;
To have them feel about me as I do about you,
To hear them say My Daddy I love you so true.

Master Bulder

Through the spoken word;
Darkness became light.
By the touch of your hands,
Living creations was birth;
From the earth, for the blind
Receive sight.

Through your eyes looking;
At the raw of nothing,
Became something in what you saw,
The master builder of all creations;
Of all nations, of all situations,
Became manifestations.

A measure of faith you've given,
Complete grace from you keeps
Us living, your mercy keeps us driven;
Your kindness sets us among the
Forgiven; our fate belongs to you,
the true master of our building.

Roses Alive

Roses need special care;
So do you and I, that's why
We must share.

Roses rise when the right
Food is fed; so do you and I
When rightly we've been led.

Encouraging words can cause
rose pedal to open wide,
encouraging words will cause
hearts to come alive.

Potter's Clay

With His hands He crafted her;
A woman from a bone call rib,
from the side of a man. In her
He placed instinct, sensitivity,
Emotions as He molded into her;
A powerful play, a nurturing spirit;
As He whittled, away with His
Clay, the beauty of it all was, the
Transformation, He made in the
Sizes of pleasingly large and
Pleasantly small.

Someone Can

Dedicated to Hurting People

When you feel you can't cope;
I know someone, who can
Give you hope.
When you can't quench your thirst;
I know someone, who can heal
All your hurts.
When you feel you have lost all liberties;
I know someone, who can give
You victories.
When you have had enough of the bitter-cup;
Ask me, I know someone, who can
 Lift you up.

He can light up your darkness, and
Guide you through the night. He
Can help you through all tests;
For, He gives you His very best.
He can hold you in His hand,
While thru it all, on your feet He
Will allow you to stand.

Fearfully-wonderfully

Dedicated to all of My Granchildren all 9 of them.

You took dirt and made a human being's worth;
You shape him into a living creation, only
Your breath, you breathe into them form such
 a great formation. A seed is what you started me
from; my parents had a part in it, but they were
only humming to the beat of your drum.

Fearfully-Wonderfully, you made me;
in a secret place with dignity and grace.
No matter how man may try to re-do me,
I'm now made and there will be no trade.
You knit me together in my Mother's
womb. I thank you for my birth Room.

My Mother Said

Humble is the way, she said;
It's in the book, she always read.
Faith is not just a word, she said;
It will keep you anchored on this earth.

Forgiveness must be real, she said;
From the heart quiet and still,
Focusing on Love for all, she said,
Will bring victory into your call.

Showing mercy to others, she said;
Will transcend broken hearts to mend.
Grace is a gift from above, she said;
Appreciate it and allow it to fly; from
you as a dove.

All Is Well

I will no longer be bait;
Sitting around in wait,
I'm part of a great plan;
I will not sink in sand.

My thoughts are of a better way;
I'm reaching for it each day,
So what no one understands;
In my corner no one raises their hands.

I'm fully dressed, completely blessed;
My limp is gone, I'm not alone,
Victory is what I smell;
In my heart all is well.

The Letter That Came

Dedicate to My Christ Kingdom Church Family

People declared you were the one;
To sit upon the throne, I ask, how could
This be? One man standing in for them and
Me. As we drag you thru council, and thru
The streets, you uttered not one word;
No help did you seek. Some said,
you stood as a man in the midst of destruction,
while others said you were standing in for this
world under construction. I admit I was
deceived. I refuse to believe, until you spoke,
"it is finish." The world darken at this time,
eyes were open including mine. As a soldier
standing there at the cross, watching you die
for all that's lost, I began a journey on that
day, in a very special way; my stance changed
from at, as a loss, to a soldier of the cross.

Peer Pressur; Just Praise Through It

Peer Pressure, Peer Pressure;
don't let it get you down;
Peer Pressure, Peer Pressure,
Will always be around, praise
The Father above, who sends you
His love. When others say you
Gonna missed out; just tell them
what you know about, being a child
of a Royal King, you only wants, what
He's ordained. Peer Pressure turn
It into Prayer Pressure; teach your
Friends to pray each and every day,
So they want feel, all alone, for God
will hear and make them strong.
He will wrap them in His arms of Love;
Protecting them from above.

Benefits of a Mother

Up at the break of day, kneeling on her
Knees to pray; looking in on her children
with a smile, remembering what's special
about each child; preparing food with such grace,
Glowing with joy over her face.

Navigating the kids off to school,
Reminding them of the golden rule.
Her love cannot be measure, to her
Family, she is a treasure. She's the
Apple of their eye, for they know she
Receives her assignments from on high.

When life's ship hits a stop; the
Fragrants of her prayers is steady as
The Rock, when we circuvent, her
Loves grows to a greater extent;
The benefits we received from her
Gentle touch, to us is what means so much.

Our Good

We've traveled over life's roads, we've carried heavy loads;
times got hard, we pray that God would not depart,
when we know not what we should pray, the spirit
itself intercedes, we hope for that we see not, for we wait
patiently. For we know, all things work together for our good.
Yeah!

We serve an able God, he design us to fit his plan, while
in his will, at his feet we stand, we are called according to His
purpose; we are called to share His word, tho storms get rough,
we know Jesus is more than enough. For we know, all things
work together for our good. Yeah!

Joy Comes

Dedicated to Pastors Van & Jackie Alexander

Stop weeping, start leaping;
For Joy is soon to come.
Stop sighing, start riding,
The wave of the storm.
It's time for you to reap
What your soul doth seek.

Joy cometh, joy cometh.
In the morning light,
Even through the night.
You will feel the joy,
Your will it will employ.

It will take over the atmosphere,
And run away your fear.
In the midst of life storms,
You will see that joy comes.

Not Today

Not seeking the status as a celebrity,
The actions of a woman stating the word
No, started a movement of unity. Her
Thoughts on giving up her seat, were today
This will not be. Rosa's actions, on the bus,
Turned out to be from the back to the front for all
Of us. Not today must have been on the mind of
Martin Luther King, as he preach non-violence, to
Let freedom ring. Not today are words that
should always be in our thoughts, when someone
states to us, our dreams are for naught.

You can be a King or Rosa Parks, but watch out
For the fiery darts. It's up to you and I, the
Young who are strong and the old who are wise.
I'm sure over the years many people got tired,
Of staying in their place, so they began to say,
Not today to the man's face. A woman called
Moses must have thought that too, during her
Daring rescues, of her parents, along with more
Than 300 slaves, became the talk of her days.

A bounty of dead or alive was placed on her head,
But nothing could deter her away from the promise
She made, word got out against her, there was a
Dangerous plot, against all odds she did not stop.
No more should we accept just anything presented
To us, for our dreams is still riding in that seat of
life's bus. So be at ease, guard your place, meet life
head on face to face, when adversity, comes your
way, let your answer be, Not Today, Not Today!